Pets

THIS EDITION
Editorial Management by Oriel Square
Produced for DK by WonderLab Group LLC
Jennifer Emmett, Erica Green, Kate Hale, *Founders*

Editors Grace Hill Smith, Libby Romero, Maya Myers, Michaela Weglinski;
Photography Editors Kelley Miller, Annette Kiesow, Nicole DiMella;
Managing Editor Rachel Houghton; **Designers** Project Design Company;
Researcher Michelle Harris; **Copy Editor** Lori Merritt; **Indexer** Connie Binder; **Proofreader** Larry Shea;
Reading Specialist Dr. Jennifer Albro; **Curriculum Specialist** Elaine Larson

Published in the United States by DK Publishing
1745 Broadway, 20th Floor, New York, NY 10019

Copyright © 2023 Dorling Kindersley Limited
DK, a Division of Penguin Random House LLC
24 25 26 27 28 10 9 8 7 6 5 4 3 2 1
001–341623–Mar/2024

A catalog record for this book
is available from the Library of Congress.
ISBN: 978-0-5938-4166-2

DK books are available at special discounts when purchased in bulk for sales promotions, premiums, fundraising, or educational use. For details, contact: DK Publishing Special Markets, 1745 Broadway, 20th Floor, New York, NY 10019
SpecialSales@dk.com

Printed and bound in China

The publisher would like to thank the following for their kind permission to reproduce their images:
a=above; c=center; b=below; l=left; r=right; t=top; b/g=background

123RF.com: Anatolii Tsekhmister / tsekhmister 12bc, 23bl; **Dreamstime.com:** Adogslifephoto 19br, Lars Christensen 7b, Alexandr Ermolaev 15bc, Linda Erwe 18br, Sonya Etchison 19bl, Eric Isselee / Isselee 6bc, Isselee 1b, 11bc, 15br, 23clb, Duncan Noakes 10-11, Irina Orlova 8-9, Svand 14-15, Shannon Tidwell 4-5; **Fotolia:** Eric Isselee1e 3cb; **Getty Images:** DigitalVision / Oliver Rossi 21br, EyeEm / Ronnachai Palas 21bl, Moment / Catherine Falls Commercial 8br, Westend61 18-19; **Getty Images / iStock:** Nattapong Assalee 12-13, E+ / JLBarranco 14br, E+ / Michele Pevide 16-17, E+ / SolStock 22; S**hutterstock.com:** Chrisbrignell 9bl

Cover images: *Front:* **Dreamstime.com:** Tartilastock (Dogsx2), Valiva ca;
Shutterstock.com: D-sign Studio 10 cla, miniwide cl, Marta Sher crb, Malinovskaya Yulia (b/g)

All other images © Dorling Kindersley
For more information see: www.dkimages.com

www.dk.com

Pets

Libby Romero

There are many kinds of pets.

Fish are pets.
Fish swim
in a tank.

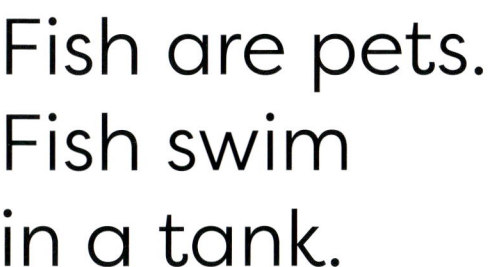

fish

Hamsters are pets.
They can run
in circles.

hamster

A hermit crab
can be a pet.
It lives in a shell.

hermit crab

This rabbit is a pet.
It hops fast.

rabbit

These birds sing.
They are pets, too.

bird

My friend has a
pet guinea pig.
It is a very furry pet!

guinea pig

I have a pet dog.
My dog does tricks.

dog

Woof! Woof!

My aunt has
lots of kittens.
She likes to
play with them.

Meow!

kittens

Meow!

People love their pets.
Pets are part
of the family!

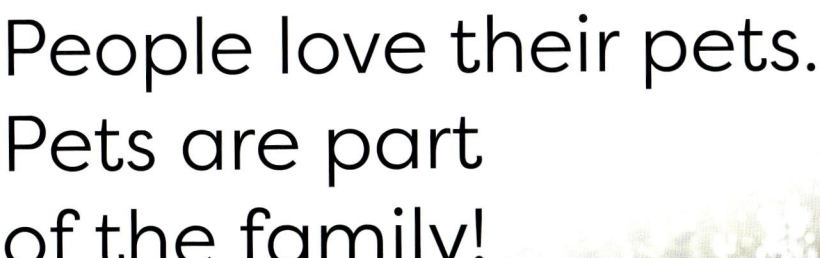

Glossary

bird
an animal with wings and a body covered with feathers

fish
a scaly animal with fins and gills that lives in the water

hamster
a small, furry animal with a round body and large pouches in its cheeks

hermit crab
a crab that lives in an empty shell to protect itself

rabbit
an animal with long ears and long hind legs

Quiz

Answer the questions to see what you have learned. Check your answers with an adult.

1. Which pet lives in a tank of water?

2. Which pet lives in a shell?

3. Which pet can hop?

4. Which pet can do tricks?

5. What is your favorite kind of pet? Why?

1. A fish 2. A hermit crab 3. A rabbit
4. A dog 5. Answers will vary

Ocean
Animals

THIS EDITION
Editorial Management by Oriel Square
Produced for DK by WonderLab Group LLC
Jennifer Emmett, Erica Green, Kate Hale, *Founders*

Editors Grace Hill Smith, Libby Romero, Michaela Weglinski;
Photography Editors Kelley Miller, Annette Kiesow, Nicole DiMella;
Managing Editor Rachel Houghton; **Designers** Project Design Company;
Researcher Michelle Harris; **Copy Editor** Lori Merritt; **Indexer** Connie Binder;
Proofreader Larry Shea; **Reading Specialist** Dr. Jennifer Albro; **Curriculum Specialist** Elaine Larson

Published in the United States by DK Publishing
1745 Broadway, 20th Floor, New York, NY 10019

Copyright © 2023 Dorling Kindersley Limited
DK, a Division of Penguin Random House LLC
24 25 26 27 28 10 9 8 7 6 5 4 3 2 1
001–341623–Mar/2024

A catalog record for this book
is available from the Library of Congress.
ISBN: 978-0-5938-4166-2

DK books are available at special discounts when purchased in bulk for sales promotions, premiums,
fundraising, or educational use. For details, contact: DK Publishing Special Markets,
1745 Broadway, 20th Floor, New York, NY 10019
SpecialSales@dk.com

Printed and bound in China

The publisher would like to thank the following for their kind permission to reproduce their images:
a=above; c=center; b=below; l=left; r=right; t=top; b/g=background

123RF.com: Visarute Angkatavanich 3cb, 20br; **Alamy Stock Photo:** Paul Harris 16-17, Paul Harris 16br;
Dorling Kindersley: Linda Pitkin 31clb; **Dreamstime.com:** Steve Allen 7tr, Andreykuzmin 20-21, Isselee 8br, Izanbar 14-15bc,
Eugene Sim Junying 31cl, Neirfy 5tl, Sandra Nelson 11tr, Sandra Nelson 30cra, Stéphane Rochon 22-23;
Getty Images: 500px Prime / Grant Thomas 9tr; **Getty Images / iStock:** atese 22br, Dimitris66 31bl, Thierry Eidenweil 23cr,
fenkieandreas 20c, Gwenvidig 17tc, ifish 27bl, ifish 31clb/1, Joegolby 10-11, Jz5 30ca, KPegg 9bc, Mlharing 11c,
RomoloTavani 29br, Mireia Querol Rovira 17bc, tswinner 25br, Tatiana Dzhemileva 4-5; **Shutterstock.com:** Chris Allan 28br,
31tl, alonanola 13bl, Daniel Avram 5cr, Karel Bartik 4-5c, 10-11bc, Agung bayu 6-7bc, Beltsazar 6-7, Maciej Czekajewski 4bc,
7bc, 31bl/1, Divelvanov 12-13, Divelvanov 18-19, David Evison 12bc, Leonardo Gonzalez 8-9, Shane Gross 25bl,
Andrea Izzotti 24br, Jellyman Photography 15br, Patrik Jonson 4bl, 27bc, Tory Kallman 28-29, orifec_a31 30, orlandin 18br,
SergeUWPhoto 26br, Shane Myers Photography 14-15, Sergey Teryaev 19bl, VisionDive 13bc, 31cla, Richard Whitcombe 1bc,
wildestanimal 19bc, Wirestock Creators 9bl, Christian Wittmann 29bl, Mike Workman 26-27

Cover images: *Front:* **Dreamstime.com:** Noviantoko Tri Arijanto b, Iuliia Sutiagina b/g;
Getty Images / iStock: Bullet_Chained c, ca; **Shutterstock.com:** VectorShow cra;
Back: **Dreamstime.com:** Punnawich Limparungpatanakij cra; **Getty Images / iStock:** Bullet_Chained clb;
Spine: **Getty Images / iStock:** Bullet_Chained

All other images © Dorling Kindersley
For more information see: www.dkimages.com

www.dk.com

Pre-level

Ocean
Animals

Ruth A. Musgrave

Many animals live in
the ocean.
Meet some of them.

Race to the water with this baby sea turtle.
A bird is chasing it.
Go turtle go!

baby sea turtle

Ride the waves with
a sea lion.
Twist. Turn. Jump.
Watch out
for that
big wave!

sea lion

This bird dives into the water. It swims fast!

penguin

Swim with this fish.
But you will have to
find it first.

frogfish

whale shark

This big shark gulps
little fish.
Open wide.

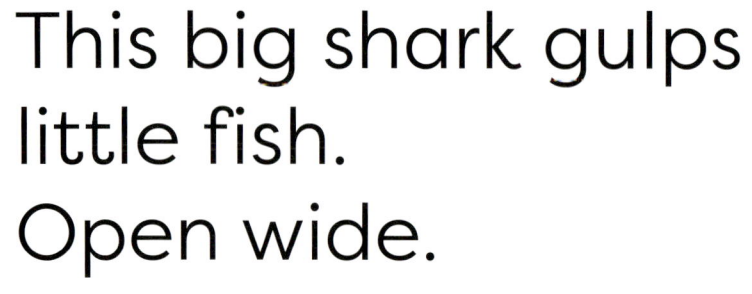

Set sail with this jelly.
It needs the wind to push it.
Blow wind blow!

by-the-wind sailor

nautilus

Look at this animal.
It has a big shell.
The shell helps it
go up.
Then down.

Stinky slime covers
this fish.
The slime tastes bad.

mandarinfish

That way other animals
will not eat this fish.

decorator crab

Dress like this crab.
Put on some rocks.
Put on some shells.
Now no one
can see you.

These fish ride on a ray.
The ray keeps
the fish safe.
The fish keep the ray
clean. Hang on!

remora fish

manta ray

Hide with a horse.
A seahorse of course.

seahorse

Jump and play.
It is the best part
of the day.

dolphin

Splash down.
Then jump again.

You did it!
You jumped. You ate.
You played like
an ocean animal.

Glossary

dolphin
a mammal that lives in the sea

frogfish
a fish that blends in with rocks or other things to hide

nautilus
a sea animal related to octopus and squid

seahorse
a fish that hides in coral

sea turtle
an animal that hatches on land, then grows up in the sea

Quiz

Answer the questions to see what you have learned. Check your answers with an adult.

1. How does the jelly move?

2. What animal has a shell?

3. Which fish stinks?

4. What animal puts on shells and rocks?

5. How do the fish help the ray?

1. The wind pushes it 2. Nautilus 3. Mandarinfish 4. Decorator crab 5. The fish keep the ray clean

Garden
Friends

FIRST EDITION

Series Editor Deborah Lock; **Senior Art Editor** Tory Gordon-Harris;
Design Assistant Sadie Thomas; **US Editor** Elizabeth Hester;
Pre-Production Producer Nadine King; **Producer** Sara Hu; **Jacket Designer** Natalie Godwin;
Publishing Manager Bridget Giles; **Reading Consultant** Linda Gambrell, PhD

THIS EDITION

Editorial Management by Oriel Square
Produced for DK by WonderLab Group LLC
Jennifer Emmett, Erica Green, Kate Hale, *Founders*

Editors Grace Hill Smith, Libby Romero, Michaela Weglinski;
Photography Editors Kelley Miller, Annette Kiesow, Nicole DiMella;
Managing Editor Rachel Houghton; **Designers** Project Design Company;
Researcher Michelle Harris; **Copy Editor** Lori Merritt; **Indexer** Connie Binder;
Proofreader Larry Shea; **Reading Specialist** Dr. Jennifer Albro;
Curriculum Specialist Elaine Larson

Published in the United States by DK Publishing
1745 Broadway, 20th Floor, New York, NY 10019

Copyright © 2024 Dorling Kindersley Limited
DK, a Division of Penguin Random House LLC
24 25 26 27 28 10 9 8 7 6 5 4 3 2 1
001–341623–Mar/2024

A catalog record for this book
is available from the Library of Congress.
ISBN: 978-0-5938-4166-2

DK books are available at special discounts when purchased
in bulk for sales promotions, premiums, fundraising, or
educational use. For details, contact: DK Publishing Special Markets,
1745 Broadway, 20th Floor, New York, NY 10019
SpecialSales@dk.com

Printed and bound in China

The publisher would like to thank the following for their kind permission to reproduce their images:
a=above; c=center; b=below; l=left; r=right; t=top; b/g=background

123RF.com: Eric Isselee / isselee 5b; **Dorling Kindersley:** Peter Anderson / RHS Hampton Court Flower Show 2014 4-5t;
Dreamstime.com: Eric Isselee 31clb, Lindavostrovska 14br, 15b; **Shutterstock.com:** hwongcc 29bl, 29br, iamharin 4c,
irin-k 10-11b, LapailrKrapai 30, SNEHIT PHOTO 6-7
All other images © Dorling Kindersley

www.dk.com

Garden Friends

butterfly

garden

Meet the small animals in the garden.

praying mantis

antennae

flower

butterflies

Hello, butterfly.
You are resting
on a flower.

wing

leaf

eye

mouth

**caterpillars**

Hello, caterpillars.
You are eating
big leaves.

spot

 **ladybugs**

Hello, ladybugs.
You have
many spots.

head

leg

head

spiders

Hello, spider.
You have spun
a big web.

web

flower

furry body

 **bumblebees**

Hello, bumblebee.
You are drinking
from a flower.

Hello, centipede.
You have many legs.

centipedes

head

leg

Hello, dragonfly. You are flying around very fast.

dragonflies

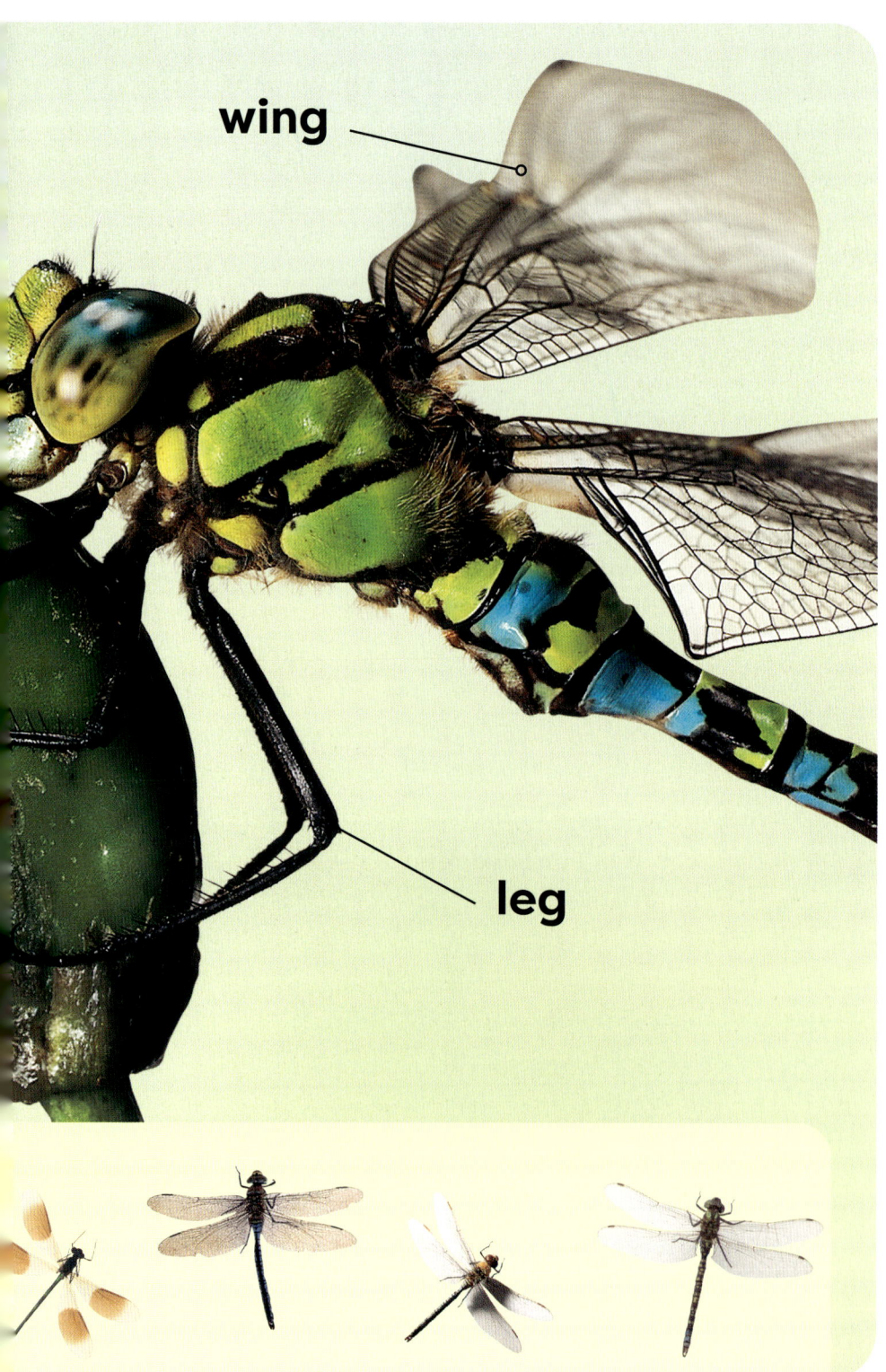

wing

leg

baby snail

shell

snails

Hello, snail.
You have a baby
on your back.

soft body

worms

Hello, worms.
You are very long.

Hello, stag beetle.
You have very
sharp jaws.

wing

beetles

head

jaws

Hello, frogs.
You are hiding
in the grass.

foot

frogs

grasshoppers

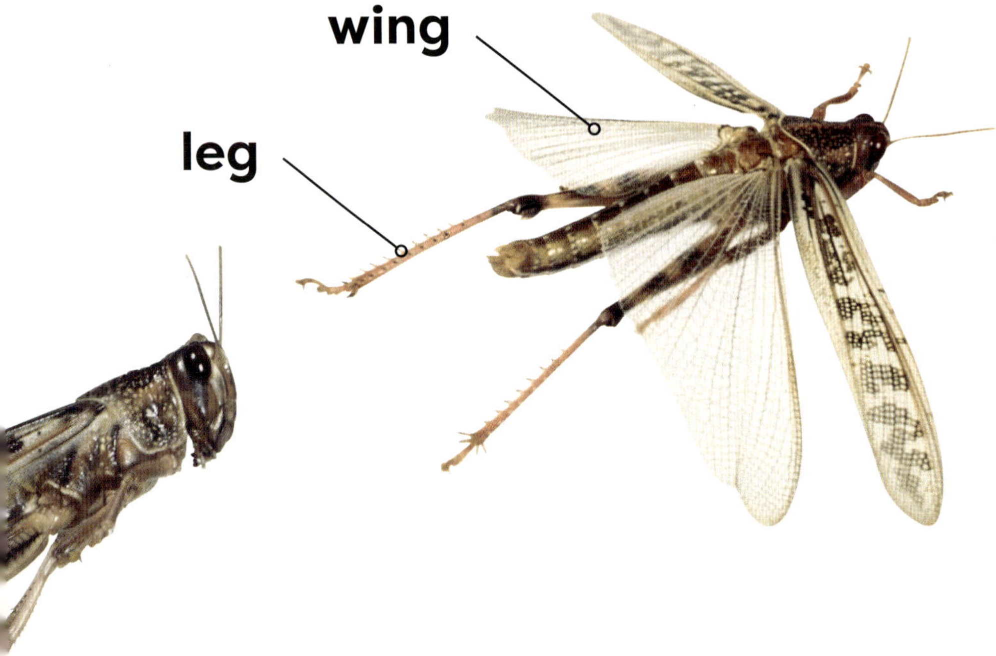

wing

leg

Hello, grasshoppers.
Wow!
What a big jump!

What animals can you find outside?

Glossary

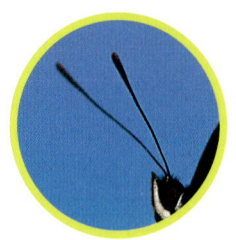

antennae
are used by insects to
feel their surroundings

centipede
an insect with
many legs

jaws
are used by stag beetles
to fight and nip

praying mantis
a bright green insect
with long front legs

web
something that some
spiders make to catch
prey and rest

Quiz

Answer the questions to see what you have learned. Check your answers with an adult.

Which animal am I?

1. I have many spots.
2. I drink from flowers.
3. I have very sharp jaws.
4. I have a soft body.
5. I move around by taking big jumps.

1. A ladybug 2. A bumblebee 3. A stag beetle
4. A worm 5. A grasshopper